# Buying Your First Horse

## How to Make an Informed Choice

# Susan Williamson

**HighTide**
Publications, Inc.

**Deltaville Virginia**

High Tide Publications, Inc.
1000 Bland Point
Deltaville, Virginia 23043
www.hightidepublications.com

First Edition


ISBN: 978-1-945990-52-6

# Table of Contents

## Notes

# Chapter 1
# Why Buy?

I just want my child to learn how to ride a horse… I don't know if I should actually buy one!

The best answer to this question was given by a mother who had spent several thousands of dollars in purchasing and training a show horse for her daughter. When asked how she could justify this expense, she answered, "It's cheaper than drug rehab."

Kids who spend their days at the barn are not spending their day at the mall, in front of video games, or texting. They learn responsibility and self-esteem by hands on experience. I had one mother tell me, "I like who she is when she comes to the barn."

*So, as long as I have somewhere for the horse to live this should be easy, right?*

*Wrong.*

Would-be horse owners need to know that a horse is not a big dog. It is a large animal which requires daily attention from someone. A horse owner is making a commitment to care for a horse or pay for its care, potentially for many years. (**See** *Chapter 9: Do Horses Live Forever?*)

I am convinced that loving horses in an incurable condition, the result of a recessive genetic trait. I've heard from parents who never even thought about a horse, but their child wants to ride and nothing else will do. I've taught beginners in their sixties who always wanted to ride, but never had the opportunity until retirement. Their desire to ride and perhaps even to own a horse has not diminished in all of that time.

So when your horse crazy daughter, son, wife or self wants a horse, what do you do?

## First: purchase riding lessons.

Riding lessons will help determine if the horse lover is serious about wanting a horse. Depending on where you live, there may be several types of riding instruction available.

### There are different ways to ride?

Western, saddle seat, dressage and hunt seat are all different ways of riding. Once you choose a style of riding, stick with it until you learn the basics. Trying out another style is fine, once you learn how to ride, but changing disciplines during the learning process will only lead to confusion.

> *Our family will just go out on trail rides for now.*
> *That should be good enough to get used to a horse.*

Renting a horse on a trail ride is not a substitute for riding lessons. Rental horses are trained to follow the horse in front of them, more or less despite what the rider does. The rider may be able to sit on a horse, but he or she receives no real training on how to control the horse and what to do in unexpected situations.

There comes a time when every horse lover wants his or her very own horse. Basic riding skills are important. But knowing how to groom, lead, tack up and generally care for a horse is also important. Many lesson programs incorporate these skills into their lessons, although you may need to request this type of instruction.

Unless you are considering a lead line pony for a small child, a rider should be able to control the horse at a walk and trot (or rack or running walk or other gait in the case of a non-trotting horse) before any thought is given to purchasing or leasing a horse.

## Horses can be leased? Really?

Yes, leases are available. They usually require that the horse remain stabled with a trainer or instructor, but leasing can be a good first step. When we operated a riding program, we often leased lesson horses. The leasee would notify us if she wanted to ride on a particular day and the horse would be reserved. On other days the horse could be used for lessons. We only charged half of regular board and the horse was worked regularly. This provided a fairly inexpensive lease, but not all stables are willing to do this. Occasionally a horse is advertised for partial or shared lease. This is a case in which the owner has limited time and is willing to share his or her use of the horse. The horse would remain in its current location.

### But leasing is just for regular horses, right?

Even top level show horses can be leased. Like any business transaction, a lease should include a signed contract spelling out the terms and the responsibilities of each party. Mortality and loss of use insurance may be required and provides protection to both parties.

Although most horse lovers want to ride their horses, driving a horse or pony to a cart or buggy is another option. Physical limitations may make it difficult for a person to ride, but driving might be an option. Some, but not all, lesson programs offer driving lessons.

Horses can be driven in shows, on suitable trails and cross country, provided one has the proper equipment and the horse has been schooled appropriately.

## Other Considerations When Buying a Horse

The decision to buy needs to include where the horse will be kept and by whom. The options include your own few acres (**See** *Chapter 8: What Does a Horse Need?*), a boarding stable or a training and boarding facility. Boarding facilities come in all shapes and sizes. Some offer only the place and the owner supplies the feed and labor. Partial board might include hay and pasture while full board would include feed and care with or without a stall. In a training facility, the horse is cared for and trained with no input required by the owner than paying the bill. The owner rides or drives or sees the horse worked by appointment.

# Chapter 2
# Now or Later: Timing Is Everything

I remember climbing into my daddy's lap and begging for a pony when I was five or six. He told me we had nowhere to keep it. Little did I know he and my mother were already searching for the farm where I would grow to adulthood.

So, once they bought the farm they bought me a pony, one of many horses I would grow to know and love over the years. My father was an experienced horseman who, unbeknownst to me, had owned and showed horses for years. When I was in seventh grade they gave me a retired show horse that could no longer compete due to breathing problems.

I was ready.

I know how much horses have meant to me and to our family over the years. I have seen young people develop confidence and responsibility through horse ownership. I would encourage anyone who truly wants a horse to make it happen.

As a riding instructor, I frequently met people who had a bad experience with a horse and were consequently terrified. They had been put on a horse or given a horse by someone who had no experience and received no instruction or guidance. No wonder bad things happened.

I have seen good riders blossom into wonderful horsemen and women once they had their own horse. But I have also seen horses languish in the pasture and children lose interest because no one has the time or expertise to help. And, I have seen well-meaning parents purchase a horse for the daughter going off to college who has no time and other interests. What might have been her dream a few years earlier receives little attention.

> *If your child (or you) is riding (or driving) competently, and if you are able and willing to provide the cost of keeping a horse and the time to enjoy it, then by all means go for it. Good judgement and patience will be required to find the right horse.*

Horses are often cheaper in the fall. Pastures fail and owners are looking to unload before they have to buy feed. This used to be true of show horses as well as backyard horses, but year round competitions have changed this timing for show animals. The fall is often the time when trainers are looking to find a new horse for their customer so as to have the team of horse and rider ready for the next competition year.

Camps and trail ride businesses may sell off their horses in the fall, rather than keep them over the winter. Individuals, too, may decide to part with their trail horse before having to purchase winter feed.

And once in a while a horse you have seen and admired may suddenly come on the market because the rider is going off to college or pursuing other interests. Be cautious, and make sure the horse isn't for sale due to a soundness problem. (**See** *Chapter 7: Buyer Beware: Help is Out There.*)

# Chapter 3
# Do Look a Gift Horse in the Mouth

## Like free lunches, there are no such things.

As soon as it becomes known that your child or niece or whomever is looking for a horse, someone may offer a free horse.

The cost of keeping a horse over time is usually greater than the purchase price. *Economics dictates it should be a horse worth keeping.*

The slant of a horse's teeth increases with age. So looking in a horse's mouth is more than a cliché. If your gift horse is too old to be useful, you are inheriting someone else's problem.

## A young, untrained horse will require many hours and dollars.

*Say "No thank you."*

In a very few instances, a rider may have outgrown his horse or pony and be willing to give or sell it very cheaply to insure a good home for a trusted equine. How old is the animal? Is it still sound and useful? If so, wonderful, but **be very cautious.**

## To rescue or not to rescue?

If a horse has been rescued, evaluated and trained over a period of many months by a professional, this might be an option. But rescue horses were sent to auction or abandoned for a reason. It may have been economic, it may have been an injury, but it may also have been dangerous behavior. The horse that has been starved may be very compliant until it consumes some groceries. Then his true nature may show up.

Many bad behaviors are the result of poor training and handling, but that doesn't mean they can always be overcome.

Another problem with rescues and adopted mustangs is parasites. Sometimes these animals have been so damaged by worms and/or disease that their life span and future health is in jeopardy. Also, they will always have some memory of their earlier life. A horse that has run wild with a herd will want to take off when he sees other horses gallop by. A horse that was abused may always panic at a stimulus reminding him of that abuse.

And, the horse may not be suitable for the type of riding or riding level of the recipient. So the "free" doesn't really matter if you end up paying thousands of dollars in maintenance for a horse that benefits no one.

A horse that has been simply turned out to pasture may take several months of retraining to be suitable for a novice rider. He may also have suffered from founder or laminitis. This condition is often caused by allowing a horse to eat too much grass or grain. It can also be caused by stress or a high fever. Once foundered, the horse will always be at risk for additional attacks and will require careful diet management and hoof care to remain sound.

Any horse you own will require care and expense. A vet check is just as important for a "free horse" as it is for a purchased horse.

Think your free horse is still a good deal? Then ask for a second opinion (**See** *Chapter 7: Buyer Beware: Help is Out There.*)

# Chapter 4
## Vices to Avoid

While horses don't smoke, drink or cuss, they can have a wide variety of other undesirable behaviors.

## Undesirable behaviors

### Cribbing

Cribbing is a vice in which a horse bites on wood and sucks air, making a strange noise. Horses can be genetically susceptible.

Why would a horse do this?

Boredom and confinement often lead to this behavior. Cribbing releases endorphins and becomes self-rewarding.

The problem with cribbers is that the behavior makes a horse much more likely to suffer from colic, **a potentially fatal gastrointestinal problem**. A cribber often wears a leather or leather and metal collar which prevents them from swallowing air when they suck on the wood. Veterinary research has shown a connection between cribbing and ulcers, but there has been no definite ruling on which is cause and which is effect.

Cribbers can be useful horses, but they will always have a greater risk of colic and require careful management.

### Weaving

Weaving is a condition in which horses perpetually pace back and forth, usually in a stall, but in some cases in pasture as well. Weavers often forget to eat and will work off many calories with this behavior. It may be hard to keep them in good flesh.

### Biting and Nipping

All horses have teeth. Therefore all horses can bite. But a horse that bites maliciously at people or other horses is not a good subject for a first horse.

Nipping is a lesser form of biting, often caused by too many treats. Many horses will nip when the girth is tightened or when they are nervous. This is not really a vice, but the handler needs to be aware.

### Kicking

All horses also have four feet and therefore can kick. Kicking and biting are part of the horse's normal means of protection and establishing rank. But a horse that deliberately kicks at humans is a problem. Routinely kicking at other horses is also a problem.

### Rearing

Rearing is a horse's response to unremitting pressure on the bit. Some horses are more sensitive than others. Beginners often react by pulling back, possibly causing the horse to fall over backwards on his rider. A horse in the habit of rearing is not safe.

### Barn Sour

Barn sour means that a horse will refuse to leave the barn or gate or will try to take his rider back to the barn or somewhere else. This habit can be easily corrected in its early stages, but becomes more of a problem if it is ingrained. Riders cause the problem by not making the horse go where he is asked. An experienced rider can handle a barn sour horse, but this is not the best first horse.

### Bucking

Bucking means kicking up with the rear legs. Some horses buck when they are feeling frisky, but others buck as a deliberate way to dislodge a rider and avoid work. Bucking broncos do not make good pleasure horses.

### Bolting

Bolting or running off is another vice. Horses are prey and are designed to flee from their predators. But a well-trained horse should not take off in response to fear or other stimulus.

### Poor Ground Manners

Poor ground manners mean that a horse is head strong—pulling, refusing to stand, rubbing on the handler. Any horse can and should be taught to walk beside the person leading him, to stop and stand quietly and to keep his head to himself. He should be willing to stand tied (with a halter and lead—never a bridle). I am always amazed at the horse owners who allow their horses to pull them wherever. Poor ground manners can be corrected over time, but they are annoying and potentially dangerous.

If your horse will be kept in a pasture, he or she needs to be easy to catch. There is nothing more annoying than being ready to ride and then being unable to catch your horse. Some horses are fine by themselves but timid in a herd, and will walk or run away if another horse approaches. This is not necessarily a deal breaker, but it does not lead to good horse/owner relationships. If the horse receives a handful of grain or a treat every time he comes in, he may be more willing. **Caution:** never enter a pasture with a visible bucket of grain lest you be mobbed.

If you plan to haul your horse to trail rides, shows or other events, be sure to find out if your prospective purchase loads willingly and hauls well. And a side note, if you will also be purchasing a horse trailer, it needs to be tall enough for your horse. Some horses walk willingly into a two horse trailer, while others are only willing to enter an open stock trailer.

## How do I avoid buying a horse with one of these problems?

Buy from a reputable person and ask for the advice of your instructor. (**See** *Chapter 7: Buyer Beware: Help is Out There*) Ask why the horse is for sale. Observe the horse in his stall or pasture. Watch while the horse is led, groomed and tacked up. Make sure you see the owner or someone ride the horse and perform all of its gaits, both in a confined area and out in the open.

If you are buying a horse to drive, obviously you need to see the horse perform under harness. Never assume that a good riding horse can be driven or vice-versa. Each discipline involves specific training. But buying a horse which is suitable to ride and drive could mean that more members of the family are able to enjoy the horse.

# Chapter 5
## Sex, Age and Breed

I will begin with sex because:

## Only breeding farms need stallions.

This is not to say that experienced riders shouldn't choose to own and ride a stallion in certain pursuits, but **a stallion is never appropriate for a child or novice rider**. This includes ponies, minis and young horses.

Some people prefer geldings (castrated males) because they tend to be even tempered. Mares can sometimes be the victims of their hormones and act a bit cranky when in heat. But mares are also maternal and are often very careful with their riders. So either can be fine for a first horse, it depends on the individual.

When we operated our own barn, I was always getting calls like this:

> *"We just bought our daughter a two year old stud colt, figured they could grow up together."*

## NO!

Young horses require training just as young riders do, and you cannot train them together. **And no stallions.**

A first horse needs to be mature, seasoned. Anywhere from six to eighteen might be a good age assuming the horse is sound, well trained and in good condition. Many of the best horses we ever owned were ten or over when we purchased them and went on to provide many more years of service.

You will hear different breeds described as hot blooded, warm blooded or cold blooded. This has nothing to do with their body temperature and everything to do with their temperament.

## Hot Blooded Breeds

- American Saddlebreds
- Arabians
- Hackneys
- Morgans
- Paso Finos
- Tennessee Walking Horses
- Standardbreds
- Thoroughbreds

and several other breeds are known as hot-blooded horses. They are responsive and interactive. They may prance and dance but remain under perfect control.

## Warm Blooded Breeds

Warm bloods are often horses whose ancestors were crossed between hot and draft breeds. They have style and collection but are heavier built than their hot blooded relatives.

- Friesians
- Dutch Warmbloods
- Hanoverians

- Andusians

and others are purebreds are often considered warmbloods. Crossbred horses can be certified as warmbloods through an inspection process.

## Cold Blooded Breeds

- Quarter horses
- Paints (a spotted horse with Quarter horse ancestry and characteristics)
- Appaloosas

are sometimes referred to as cold blooded horses. They tend to be calmer and quieter than the hot blooded and warm blooded horses. They can be slow and plodding or quick and athletic depending on their training and conformation. An Appendix Quarter horse is the result of a Thoroughbred/Quarter Horse cross and may share more of the Thoroughbred disposition as well as speed and other characteristics.

## Pintos

Pintos are spotted horses which may be of any breed or cross. There is a Pinto registry, with the requirement that the horse have color and at least one registered parent. In the United States any spotted horse can be a pinto, but Paint refers to a breed.

## Draft Horses

Draft horses are horses bred for heavy work—Belgians, the famous Budweiser Clydesdales, and Shires are a few. There are also draft pony breeds such as Halflingers. While draft horses are often quiet and gentle, their sheer size makes them less than suitable as first horses—think broken toes and feet, not to mention their increased feed consumption. The draft pony breeds, however, can sometimes make great beginner mounts if they are well trained.

Remember that they are very strong and if they are willful that can be problem for a young rider.

These are general descriptions, but for specifics go to the breed association websites.

## Ponies

And speaking of ponies—a good pony is hard to beat and harder to find. Ponies tend to be mischievous and many have been allowed to do as they please. Because someone can lead a child on a pony does not mean it is broke for children to ride.

By definition a pony is an equine smaller than 14 or 14.2 hands. Some small breeds such as Icelandic horses and Caspian horses are below that size but referred to as horses. A well trained pony between 11 and 14 hands can be a wonderful first mount because their size makes them easier for a child to handle, yet they are large enough for a small adult to ride if correction is needed. Popular pony breeds include:

- Shetlands
- Welsh
- POA (Pony of the Americas—an Appaloosa type pony)
- Connemara

Hackney ponies are very hot blooded and would more likely be suitable for driving, although they are shown under saddle by good riding kids. They might not make the best backyard pony for the novice rider.

If a pony is trained to ride and drive, it would be suitable for children to ride and both children and adults to drive.

Very tiny ponies, referred to as minis or miniature horses, are usually not suitable children's mounts.

They often carry dwarf genes and may not be well proportioned.

And since no adult can ride them, they may not be well trained. Minis may be trained to drive, however, and enjoyed by both children and adults.

Different breeds of horses were bred for different characteristics and purposes with certain traits selected over time. As a result, certain breeds excel at certain jobs, but individuals may prove the exception.

## Training is key

A horse of any breed or cross can be a wonderful first horse if it is well trained and good natured.

The individual horse's disposition and training is the important thing. But so often I hear that someone's first horse was so ill mannered that it frightened him or her and put them off riding for life. How sad. Or, it may have been totally ill-suited for the type of riding that the rider wished to pursue. This only leads to discouragement.

## Certain breeds are beter suited to certain styles of riding

While there are versatile horses in all breeds, some breeds and individuals are better suited to certain styles of riding or driving. Will you want to trail ride? Compete in 4-H, Pony Club or saddle club shows? A little self -education is helpful here.

Attend a few horse events and make note of the different breeds and styles. Many shows are breed specific while others are open to all breeds.

Talk to riding instructors in your chosen discipline.

## How do you choose a discipline and hence the correct horse?

Riding lessons are a start. We tend to divide riding styles into English and Western.

### English Riding Style

An English saddle does not have a horn.

English style includes saddle seat, hunt seat, dressage. Within those disciplines are further classifications. In English style riding, the rider learns to post the trot—rising and falling in time with the horse's diagonal motion. Some breeds do not trot— Tennessee Walking horses, Missouri Fox Trotters, Racking horses and Paso Finos to name a few. The rider often uses an English saddle but there is no need to post. The horse performs a two beat lateral gait or four beat gait which does not bounce the rider. American Saddlebred horses can be trained to perform five gaits. A five-gaited horse trots, but also performs a slow gait and rack, both of which are smooth four beat gaits distinguished by the speed and timing.

Saddle seat is similar to the classical seat with an erect posture. Hunt seat is designed for jumping and is sometimes referred to as forward seat since the rider leans forward when taking a jump. Dressage is an erect seat used for performing precise maneuvers.

### Western Style Riding

Western style riding involves a saddle with a horn.

The rider does not usually post because the horses best suited for western riding usually have a slow, soft trot known as a jog. Just as there are different classifications of English riding, western pleasure is very different from barrel racing, roping, team penning, reining and other western pursuits.

The horse doesn't care what type of saddle he is wearing as long as it fits.

He does care about how the rider cues him and uses the bridle to communicate with him. He will have been trained with a particular type of bit and specific cues.

### Driving

Driving can be a trot across the field in a small cart, competitive with obstacles on a course, cross county on suitable trails or in a variety of divisions in horse shows.

### Trail riding

Trail riding can be done using any breed, any style of riding. The important thing is a well-behaved, responsive horse that doesn't spook easily. The horse needs to be surefooted and good thinking.

Most horse people have favorite breeds and styles of riding and will try to steer you in their direction. Visit a few barns and a few events to look for the type of riding you or your child wishes to do.

## Notes

# Chapter 6
# How Much $$$

## How much does a horse cost?

Horses can range in price from a few hundred dollars to more than a million. In the case of race horses, several million may be spent on a young horse. One horse can win well over a million dollars and a successful breeding stallion could earn millions more over his breeding career.

## What should you expect to spend for your first horse?

Since the cost of horse training is significant, untrained horses are the cheapest, but **you don't want to go there**.

The cost of keeping a horse over time usually equates to more than the purchase price. (**See** *Chapter 8: What Does a Horse Need?*)

It makes sense to buy a horse that is worth keeping, a horse that suits the rider's skill level and purpose.

An older horse, fifteen or more, if he is sound and well cared for, may have many years of useful life ahead of him. Such a horse will tend to be cheaper than a younger model.

Although we don't have horse slaughter plants operating in the United States at the moment, horses are purchased at auction to be hauled to Mexico for slaughter, and this market sets a base price for horseflesh. Supply and demand is in play. And, like any item for sale, the price is often determined by how badly the owner wishes to sell.

You can expect to pay anywhere from $1,000 to $5,000 for a suitable, well trained horse or large pony between the ages of seven and fifteen. You might find a bargain if an outgrown horse's owner is seriously concerned about a good home for their equine partner. A horse suitable for a specific discipline such as three day eventing, showing in a particular division, fox-hunting, dressage or barrel racing will most likely come at a higher price. If this seems like too much money, realize that a beef cow sells for $1200 or more and requires no training.

## What about buying a horse for competition?

If competition is your goal, the price will vary with the level of competition. A horse which can successfully compete at small shows will generally be more affordable that a horse that can compete at regional and national events. Will the horse need to remain in training for competition? This could be a considerable annual expense along with the costs of the competitions themselves.

A famous equitation instructor in our breed was known for refusing to take students below a certain income level. I found her position very snobbish until I met her.

She said:

> *"I don't want to train a student and have them disappointed because no matter how hard they work, their parents don't have the resources to buy the horse and equipment they need to be successful."*

In that context her policy made perfect sense.

Price points will vary. Be realistic about your budget and your goals. And realize that one or the other may need to be adjusted.

Talk with your instructor to determine a reasonable price for the age and type of horse you want. Look at various online listing sites for prices of different kinds of horses.

### I can just sell my horse later and get my money back, right?

Do not expect to recoup your purchase price if you decide to sell the horse in the future. Used cars decrease in value and so do used horses, unless the horse becomes more valuable due to success in a competitive venue.

People sometimes expect to sell a horse for the price they paid even after the horse has developed a soundness problem or a behavior issue. Just as in operating a car, you have received value for the years you have owned the horse and that's the way you need to look at the economics of ownership.

### We love THIS horse but she's too expensive...

If the asking price of a suitable horse seems too high, there may be some alternatives. The seller may be willing to take payments. Bartering can work. A seller may accept labor or goods as a partial payment. When I was growing up my father accepted a new dishwasher, a chair, several old carriages and various forms of labor as partial payment for horses. If you already own a horse of some type, you may be able to trade it in on the new horse.

Many stables have programs where youth or adults can work to earn riding lessons or offset board or show expenses.

Labor may also be traded for board in private situations. Our daughter's boarder pays no fees, but feeds once a day, helps with hay pickup and horse sits when the family is out of town. A win/win for both parties and their horses.

## Notes

# Chapter 7
# Buyer Beware: Help Is Out There

## What if I unknowingly buy a horse with problems?

Unfortunately, there isn't a "Lemon Law" for horses. Unscrupulous sellers may misrepresent a horse in terms of age, soundness, behavior, etc. Other sellers may misrepresent a horse out of ignorance. Either way can be disaster for the novice buyer.

## Steer away from horse auctions.

Only experienced or professional horsemen should ever buy a horse at auction.

When you go to look at a horse, it may be sedated to appear calm, worked for hours before you see it or given painkillers to alleviate a lameness issue. This is why you need your riding instructor or another experienced person to advise you.

A knowledgeable horse person knows the preliminary questions to ask such as:

"Is this horse suitable for a beginner/novice rider?"

"How have you used the horse?"

"How long have you had the horse?"

...and so forth.

Always see the horse being ridden.

If it appears safe, your instructor or advisor should ride the horse as well. Only then should the novice try it out.

## Pre-purchase veterinary exam

A pre-purchase veterinary exam is always a good idea. If you plan to insure the horse, a veterinary exam may be required anyway. Such an exam doesn't rule out future health problems, but it can alert the buyer to any red flags. The extent of the exam may depend on the future use of the horse. X-rays are not needed for a backyard horse, but might be a good precaution for a more expensive show or other performance horse.

## Advertising Terms

When you begin searching for a horse, you may want to understand a few terms often used in advertising.

### Rides Children

I have seen ads for horses saying, "Rides children." (I hope it doesn't—it would be hard on the children.) This implies that the horse is suitable for children but really means that a child has sat on the horse with an adult holding it. This has nothing to do with the actual suitability of the horse for a novice rider.

### "Game" or "forward moving"

This means that the horse wants to go, usually fast, and might be too much for the beginner.

### "Green broke"

This means that the horse has just been started in his lessons. He can be ridden, but again is probably not a good choice for a first horse.

It is important to know what job the horse has been doing.

We once had a customer buy a barrel racing horse for his timid daughter. The horse wanted to take off like a rocket the minute you asked him to go forward. After months of training, the horse began to relax, but he was still easily spooked and managed to dismount many riders.

## Has the horse even been trained?

Just because a horse appears gentle and quiet when led, doesn't mean it has ever been properly trained.

An untrained horse should never be your first horse.

Training a horse to a level where he is safe and reliable takes many months, sometimes years. Horse training costs a minimum of $300 to $400 per month and can be over $2,000 per month, not counting extras like shoeing, vet bills, etc.

Television and movie appearances of one day clinicians are misleading. "Horse Whisperers" may have a horse quietly responding to them in one day, but do not assume that horse is trained. I had a friend who took an unbroken horse to one of these workshops then took it trail riding. She got into trouble when the horse took off and wouldn't stop.

> She asked me, "What would you do if you were on the trail with a horse that wouldn't stop?"

> I answered, "I wouldn't go on the trail with a horse that wouldn't stop."

Trail rides are for seasoned, mature horses that don't spook easily and respond to the rider's commands.

If you or your child are involved in a lesson program, your instructor is the best person to ask for help in finding a horse.

He or she knows your riding ability and may even know of

a suitable horse for sale or lease. If he or she doesn't know of an available horse, the instructor may be willing to find a horse.

## Horses are listed for sale on:

- stable websites
- horse specific websites
- breed specific websites
- general online marketing websites
- notices at your local feed store
- classified ads

Many of the online sites allow you to filter your search by breed, locality, training etc. This can give you a starting point, but nothing beats a horse that your instructor knows and feels would be suitable.

## This is all part of the instructor's job, right?

The instructor should be paid for time spent in evaluating a horse. After all, time and expertise has a value. If he or she finds the horse, usually a commission is involved, just as in buying a house. Otherwise, you need to pay his or her time and travel to go see and try out the horse. Often a phone call on the part of the instructor can rule out a particular horse, saving time for everyone concerned.

In today's digital age, horses are often advertised online and sold online via video.

Unless a professional is buying from another professional that he or she knows and trusts, this is not a good plan for the first time buyer.

Often a horse can be kept on trial for a month, especially if it is placed in the care of a trainer or instructor.

If you know people who have recently purchased a horse from a trainer or stable, ask about their experience. If you have doubts about your instructor's choice of a horse, find someone familiar with the type of riding and horse you are considering and ask for a second opinion. While most horse professionals are honest and above board, a few are not, either through ignorance or the need to sell a horse.

Unfortunately, we have had customers to bring us horses that were purchased through their trainers or instructors and were totally unsuitable or unsound. But, there are always two sides to any story and a good horse can go bad in the wrong hands very quickly.

## And finally, it is important to buy the right horse for the job.

Again that's why the advice of an expert is important. Just because a horse is sound, well broke and good at its job doesn't mean it will be good at another job. A wonderful trail horse might not be the best candidate for the show ring. A draft cross with no ground manners won't work for a small rider.

The cost of advice is small compared to the cost of buying the wrong horse

## Notes

# Chapter 8
# What Does a Horse Need?

Horses have been domesticated for thousands of years. This partnership allowed humans to benefit from having transportation and "horse power". In return, the horse was provided with feed, water and protection from predators.

> *Whether you plan to care for your horse yourself or board him at a stable, he requires daily attention from someone.*

Despite the size of horses, they can be easily injured by falls, fights with other horses or simply taking a bad step. They can jump fences, crash through gates and generally land themselves in the most absurd predicaments. (Upside down in a concrete water tank comes to mind—true story.) They can suffer colic, a severe gastrointestinal pain that requires immediate attention. And unless you have adequate pasture, **they need daily feed**.

## Where will your horse live?

First of all, a horse requires somewhere to be—ideally, a pasture with good grazing. However, horses can exist in dry lots or in stalls provided they receive plenty of roughage and exercise.

The number of acres of pasture required for one horse varies widely with the type of soil and the climate. Too much grass is as problematic as too little. Hay, alfalfa cubes and other feeds can supplement the pasture grazing, so long as most of the diet is in the form of roughage.

The pasture needs to be safely fenced with a source of fresh, clean water.

## Fences

Safe fencing can be board fence, woven wire with small blocks at the bottom, high tension wire, vinyl or electric. Barbed wire is not ideal, but in large pastures it can sometimes work, especially if horses are not on the other side. I have seen more injuries from woven wire with blocks large enough to trap a horse's foot than I have from barbed wire, but both are dangerous, especially if not well maintained.

The important thing is that the fence is kept in good repair and visible to the horse.

Horses kept in adjacent pastures may fuss over the fence or kick at it, which is why double fencing may be used. An electric wire strung at the top or inside the fence can help to prevent this behavior.

Horses learn to respect electric wire or tape, but they need to be introduced to it—allowing them to receive a mild shock so they know to stay away.

## Housing

Shade and shelter are also important, but a barn is not essential. Horses in the wild do not have barns or run-in sheds. Horses often prefer to be outside even in bitter cold or blazing sun. A few shade trees or a wooded area can provide both shade and shelter. The hardest condition for horses is freezing rain. It is difficult for them to stay warm but with plenty of hay, they can handle it.

Although horse blankets can do more harm than good, a waterproof rug or blanket can offer protection from sleet or freezing rain.

A barn is helpful in bad weather and also as a place to confine your horse for tacking up, grooming and medical attention. An injured horse may need to be confined to a stall or shed.

The shelter should be free from loose boards, nails or other projections which could injure a horse.

The ceiling should be high enough that the horse is not likely to hit his head.

## Food

If a horse is not working hard, roughage alone may be sufficient. If he is older, or working hard, he may benefit from small amount of grain. He will also need a trace mineral salt block or other source of salt. Pasture grazing may be sufficient in the summer if there is enough grass, but when grass is limited a supplement of hay is required. It should be clean and free from mold or dust. Square bales or round bales are fine, but round bales should be protected from the elements until they are fed.

## Bedding

If the horse is to be kept in a stall all or part of the time, bedding is required. This can be straw, sawdust, shavings or other suitable material that will help to keep the stall dry and give the horse some cushion. Stalls should be cleaned daily.

Devoted horse owners can't wait to buy blankets for their horses.

*Horses are not people.*

If left alone, they grow their own thick winter coats to protect them from the cold. However, if a horse has been body clipped for show or hunting or other use, he may need a blanket. Outside horses can benefit from a fly mask or even a fly sheet if insects are a problem. Show and race horses often wear sheets or blankets in their stalls to help keep their coats slick and clean.

## Basic grooming equipment

Essential equipment for the horse includes:

- A hoof pick
- halter
- lead
- saddle
- saddle pad
- girth
- bridle or hackamore (bitless bridle)
- and a bucket.

It is important to be sure the bridle and bit are similar to what the horse has been using. Often the seller may be willing to sell the horse's bridle for an additional fee. The rider needs a helmet, boots and possibly a riding crop. If driving is the intent, one needs a cart or buggy (a cart has two wheels while a buggy has four), a sturdy harness and a driving whip.

## Farriers

Horses have hooves which are similar in composition to our fingernails. The hooves grow constantly and unless the horse evenly wears them off in pasture, they require occasional trimming.

Horses wear shoes to protect their feet from hard surfaces.

Some horses have very hard hooves and don't require shoes in most circumstances. A horse ridden only on grass or sand may not require shoes. Or, he may only need shoes in front because the front feet carry more weight. In snowy, icy winters, the pastured horse will be better off without shoes because ice can build up within the shoe making it difficult for the horse to walk.

*A knowledgeable farrier can determine what your horse needs.*

A shod horse (one wearing shoes) needs to be seen by the farrier every six to eight weeks to trim the hoof and reset the shoes. Otherwise the foot will grow out over the shoe and may break off when the horse eventually loses the shoe. A barefoot horse can go a little longer between trimmings. Farrier costs vary by region and experience.

## Parasite control is essential

The frequency of deworming depends on the concentration of horses and the condition of the horse. Horses spread out in good sized pastures may only need quarterly deworming, while horses concentrated on dry lots may need monthly treatment. There are daily de-wormers, but some veterinarians and horsemen feel that these compromise the horse's immune system by removing all parasites. De-wormers are readily available in tubes and fairly easy to administer.

## Exercise is essential for a healthy horse.

If he lives in a pasture, he gets his own. But if he is confined to a stall or small dry lot, he needs to be ridden, worked or turned out frequently.

## Shots and Vaccines

Most boarding facilities require proof of negative Coggins test.

This is an annual blood test to be sure the horse does not suffer from or carry equine infectious anemia, an incurable disease. Annual vaccinations for rabies, tetanus and various infectious diseases, depending on the location, are standard. When horses are traveling to shows, twice a year influenza vaccines may be appropriate. An owner may vaccinate his or her own horse, but some vaccines are only available to veterinarians. The rules vary by state.

## Teeth

Another annual task is checking the horse's teeth to be sure they have not developed sharp points or other problems. A veterinarian or a horse dentist may need to "float" the horse's teeth. This involves manually or mechanically grinding off any sharp points, or possibly pulling a loose tooth. Some horses have well aligned teeth which rarely need intervention while others may benefit from yearly floating.

Dental care is important because teeth problems can interfere with eating, causing horses to spill their grain or be unable to properly chew their hay. A sharp point or other problem can also cause the horse discomfort when wearing the bridle and lead to behavior issues. The cost of a needed teeth floating can be recouped in feed efficiency and performance.

Veterinarians, farriers and others who come to out to work on a horse expect the owner or a caretaker to be on hand to hold the horse, give instructions and provide payment.

Boarding barns will often provide this service for a fee. If the same veterinarian or farrier is coming to a location to service several horses, the travel fee may be reduced. If an owner keeps his horse at home, he may wish to haul it to a larger barn in order to reduce costs or obtain the services of a particular practitioner.

## Horses are herd animals.

They are happiest when there are other horses nearby. This could be in the same pasture, in a neighboring pasture or within sight. A horse may be kept alone, but some horses won't thrive without company. The companion could be a donkey or a mini or one or more other horses.

If you have room, you might consider boarding additional horses as a way of offsetting costs. But bear in mind, that more horses eat more feed, make more manure, etc. Although horse lovers may use a lonely horse as an excuse to buy another horse, someone probably has an older horse that needs a home. (**See** *Chapter 9: Do Horses Live Forever?*)

## Where do you plan to ride your horse?

A child or even adult novice rider can benefit from a ring or other enclosure in which to work the horse. This could be a round pen, a ring or a small paddock. The perimeter needs to be sturdy, such as a board fence or metal fence panels. All weather footing (sand or crushed rock) is nice but not essential. Even if you plan to ride cross country, having a small fenced area can be useful to school your horse or help a young rider develop confidence.

## Boarding Facilities

If you plan to board your horse, take into account the riding facilities at the stable. Lights, a covered arena, and all weather footing can all add to the number of days and times that will be suitable for riding. If you only wish to trail ride, then such amenities are not important.

A wash area with paved or gravel footing and a hose connection is a good place to wash your horse, hose him down after a hard workout or run cold water on an injured area. You can do this in the grass of course, but unless you change locations you will end up with mud or a mud hole if your horse likes to paw. A well-equipped boarding stable may offer a wash room with hot and cold water.

## Ask what the rider needs.

If you are buying a horse for a child, he or she might be better off at a large stable where supervision is available. Do not, however, treat a boarding facility as a free babysitter. Always ask if your child may be dropped off. If the child is not capable of catching, tacking up and riding the horse without help, purchase a lesson or stay to supervise.

If you are keeping the horse at home, it is important to set ground rules for any children in the household as to when they may enter the pasture, work with the horse, etc.

Be careful to supervise visiting children who may have no knowledge of safety around horses.

# Chapter 9
# Do Horses Live Forever?

Horses and especially ponies have been known to live into their forties.

## When is a horse considered old?

A horse is considered old in the late teens, but just as human life expectancy has improved with better medical care, so has horse lifespans. The useful lifespan of a horse in good health can be well into the twenties. It all depends on care and overall health.

### Teeth

Horse's teeth are often the limiting factor. As a horse ages, his teeth wear and eventually he may not be able to chew properly, making good nutrition difficult. There are feeds designed for senior horses, but so far no false teeth.

### Injuries, arthritis and founder

Injuries, arthritis, founder (also known as laminitis) and other conditions can cause lameness, ending the useful life of a horse. If it is a mare of good bloodlines, she may be suitable for breeding. If the horse can no longer be used, are you still willing to support it? Sometimes a horse may serve as a companion horse to another horse in a pasture. The demand for companion horses or pasture ornaments is rather low.

## What to do with an old horse

If he can be used at all, you may be able to donate him to a therapeutic riding program, college riding program or other charity. If the horse is in pain or has a greatly diminished quality of life, it may be time to euthanize him. Another option is always the horse auction, but you may be consigning your faithful friend to slaughter or mistreatment.

## Horse life insurance

Horses can live a long time, longer than a dog, but unfortunately, they can also die young. Horse insurance is available for mortality and also loss of use. The cost will depend on the value of the horse and his age. A benefit for colic surgery may be included in a mortality policy. In addition major medical and surgical protection is also available. A horse can be an important part of your life for many years or can be gone all too soon.

———

If you follow the advice in this book, I hope you will end up with your forever horse, or a suitable equine companion that will bring you much joy until it is time to move up to a better, younger, or otherwise different horse. Horse ownership isn't for everyone, but horses are amazing companions.

# About the Author

**Susan Williamson** has been an extension agent, a journalist, a farmer, a gardener, an educator, and a life-long horseperson. She and her husband, Wallace, have raised, trained and shown horses for many years after they first met at a horse show. She continues to work as a substitute riding instructor.

Using her horse experience as background, she has written three mystery novels: *Turkmen Captives*—reissued as *Desert Tail, Tangled Tail*, and *Dead on the Trail* available from Amazon or from the author at susanwilliamsonnc@gmail.com. She is a member and former VP for Programs of Winston-Salem Writers and a member of Chesapeake Bay Writers. She served as editor of The Edmonton Herald-News and co-editor of the WS Writers Anthology, Flying South.

She is a graduate of the University of Kentucky with a degree in animal science and an MS from the University of California, Davis, in animal breeding and genetics.

She now lives with her husband and Labradoodle in Williamsburg, VA.

www.ingramcontent.com/pod-product-compliance
Lightning Source LLC
Chambersburg PA
CBHW021119020426
42331CB00004B/554